IT'S A MOM'S LIFE!

D1710777

NOT FOR RESALE

IT'S A MOM'S LIFE!
CARTOONS BY DAVID SIPRESS

A PLUME BOOK

BOOKS ARE AVAILABLE AT QUANTITY DISCOUNTS WHEN USED TO PROMOTE
PRODUCTS OR SERVICES. FOR INFORMATION PLEASE WRITE TO PREMIUM
MARKETING DIVISION, PENGUIN BOOKS USA INC. 375 HUDSON STREET,
NEW YORK, NEW YORK 10014.

Copyright © 1988 by David Sipress

All rights reserved

Some of the cartoons in this book appeared previously in *New Woman* and
Family Circle magazines.

REG. TRADEMARK—MARCA REGISTRADA

Library of Congress Cataloging-in-Publication Data

Sipress, David.
It's a mom's life.

1. Mothers—Anecdotes, facetiae, satire, etc.
I. Title. II. Title: It's a mom's life.
PN6231.M68S5   1988   741.5′973   87-31546
ISBN 0-452-26067-1

First Printing, April, 1988

4 5 6 7 8 9

PRINTED IN THE UNITED STATES OF AMERICA

SIPRESS

SIPRESS

Honey, why don't we at least wait until she's born before we worry about how to pay for her college education?

It was a very difficult labor.
Jeez!! I just got here, and I feel guilty already...
SIPRESS

Well, if it's not y<u>our</u> turn, and it's not <u>my</u> turn, then whose turn is it??!!

I'm sorry to bother you again, Doctor, she
seems to be all better, and she did cough
only once or twice today, but the second
time she coughed it made a funny little
noise, you know, like a whistle, and it
did only last a second, and, as I say, she
hasn't coughed again all day, but I was
a teeny bit worried, so I thought I'd
better call you, to see if you thought it
might be anything (the cough, that is),
because it's better to be safe than sorry,
but, really, she's fine, but I thought
I'd better check anyway, and, of course,
I can bring her right over there if you
think it sounds serious, but she is just
fine, there was only that funny cough...

SIPRESS

SIPRESS

SIPRESS

How did you do it, Mom? And without Sesame Street!

SIPRESS

I don't wanna! No! No! I won't go to bed! No! No! No! No! I don't want to!! I'm not gonna go! No! No! No! No! No! No!!!
Remember how happy we were that she could talk?
SIPRESS

Tell me a story about a big bear that hides under a tree, until a big fire engine comes along, and out jumps a fireman, who runs over to save the bear from an ugly purple monster, who eats them both up, and then he's still hungry, so he goes to the kitchen, and eats ten boxes of cookies, until his mommy comes home in a helicopter, and gives him lots of presents, and.....

SIPRESS

Which is sooner, Mom, tomorrow or next week?

EXERCISES FOR MOM:

THE RACE TO THE CORNER

Ideal for raising the heart rate!

SIPRESS

THE CLOTHING PICK-UP.

Builds up those biceps, especially if done consistently.

WEIGHTLIFTING (#1)

Also known as walking to the playground.

SIPRESS

WEIGHTLIFTING (#2)

Also known as pregnancy.

SIPRESS

THE FIVE-MILE PACE

Usually performed on date nights, awaiting the return of teenage son or daughter.

AEROBIC TANTRUM

(Also known as "the plate smash" when performed in the kitchen.)
It's a great workout for the whole body!!

We're celebrating: Our three-year-old went in the toilet today!

Do you think she likes the babysitter
better than she likes me??

Believe it or not, when I was a little girl there was no Tofutti.

Well... what if instead of thinking about nuclear war, you just thought about regular war?...

Grandma, when Mom was a little girl did she ever talk about me?
SIPRESS

... and then you came along, and Daddy finally had to grow up.
SIPRESS

Are you warm enough, Dear ? . . . . .

SIPRESS

They're His Children When...

... there's a slight breakdown in communication.

When...

... he decides to redecorate his room.

When...

... <u>someone</u> has to say no.

When...

... she makes a new friend.

SIPRESS

When...

SIPRESS

... he asks difficult scientific questions.

When...

SIPRESS

... he shows signs of becoming his own person.

When...

... <u>he</u> finally gets home.

SIPRESS

Don't worry, Dear, he'll grow into it.

No, Honey! Food goes in the food processor, <u>words</u> go in the word processor!

...And the next time those other kids call you "snotty little yuppies," you just explain to them that it's not right to make generalizations.

ANIMAL MOMS:

SIPRESS

It's exactly one hour since you finished your lunch, so you can go in the water now, but don't splash around, don't go out too far, don't stick your head under water, watch out for sharp rocks and shells, don't dive into the waves and knock yourself out, be careful of the undertow, don't stay in too long, and be sure to dry off immediately or else you'll get a terrible burn....

CHRISTMAS WITH MOM:

It's for you, Mom, but if there's *ever* a day when you're not using it, I thought that maybe I could borrow it....

What I'd "like" is several million dollars and a trip to Europe. But I'll settle for a scarf.

Why is it that you two see a skateboard, and I see years of constant worry?
SIPRESS

SIPRESS

And don't give me that "Einstein failed math" routine again!!
SIPRESS

Really, it's O.K., Mom. I can sleep in class tomorrow.

Mom, I'm leaving. I can't make the commitment.

The Exercise of Raw Power:

I don't need a reason:
I'm your mother!!!

SIPRESS

I'm conducting a survey: Am I a good mother?

SIPRESS

But Mom, I'm trying to stunt my growth!

Why can't I have a trust fund? All the other kids have trust funds!!
SIPRESS

Get your own apartment, Honey,
don't worry about me...

① I've been married to your father for thirty years...

② I gave up my career, my whole life for him.

③ Whatever you do, Dear, don't make my mistake and give it all up for a man.

④ So....Have you met anyone "special" lately?

SIPRESS

....Be a good boy!!...

About the Author

David Sipress, a cartoonist and sculptor, presently
lives in New York City. His work
has appeared in *New Woman, Family
Circle, Psychology Today, The Boston
Phoenix, Good Times,*
and *New Times Weekly.*

PLUME TICKLES YOUR FUNNYBONE

MAXINE! by Marian Henley. The first cartoon novel featuring the fabulous feminist and flirt, Maxine. Through her disastrous affair with the debonair T.S. Maverick and her tortured and hilarious recovery, Maxine always follows one rule—never, under any circumstances, remove your sunglasses! "Chronicles the inner flights of fancy and frenzy taken by one thoroughly modern woman."—*Utne Reader*   (259991—$6.95)

HOLLENHEAD by Sabin C. Streeter. From the happily dog-eared pages of the *Yale Daily News* comes this hilarious send-up of the college scene. "In the world of art, precocious talent is a rare commodity. Among the chosen few is Yale's Sabin Streeter, a comic strip creator extraordinaire."—*Interview*   (259541—$5.95)

THE OFFICIAL M.D. HANDBOOK by Anne Eva Ricks, M.D. Are you M.D. material? Find out with this hilarious handbook of tricks and secrets of the medical trade. Dr. Ricks offers an irreverent and humorous look at the life of a doctor, from med school to malpractice insurance.   (254388—$4.95)

THE UNOFFICIAL NURSE'S HANDBOOK by Nina Schroeder, R.N., with Richard Mintzer. Find out what makes a nurse tick! Nina Schroeder will have in stitches as she introduces you to the best and worst moments in a nursing career. From favorite nurse entertainment to famous phrases they teach in nursing school, the contents of this book are guaranteed to have you in stitches!   (258995—$6.95)

IT'S A MOM'S LIFE! by David Sipress. Faster than a speeding teenager, more powerful than a squalling toddler, able to reduce grown men to infancy with a single look . . . it's Mom! David Sipress takes a loving and whimsical look at the age-old institution of motherhood in this cartoon collection that will have you laughing page after page.   (260671—$4.95)